GIRL
ON A
MOTORCYCLE

AMY NOVESKY   Illustrated by **JULIE MORSTAD**

VIKING

PARIS, 1973

She wants to write. And to wander.
She dreams of wandering the world.
To go Elsewhere.

elsewhere /ˌɛlsˈwɛəə/ adverb
1. in or to another place; somewhere
else. Word Origin: Old English elles
hwær; see else, where

So one day the girl gets on a motorcycle and she rides away.

She wears only what she needs: a helmet, goggles, a leather jacket to keep out the wet and the cold.
She carries her life in a hand-sewn clutch and two saddlebags.

WHAT TO PACK:

✕ a good pen, a sharp knife, a blank book, lipstick

✕ a bathing suit

✕ a pretty white dress

✕ a pair of sandals

✕ a toothbrush

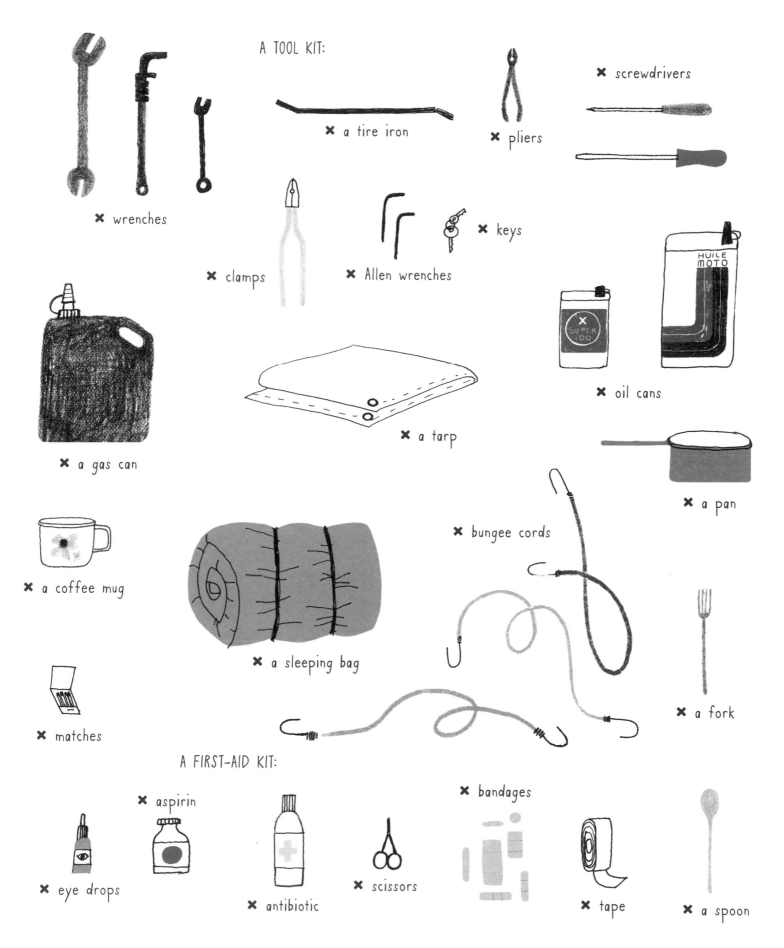

A TOOL KIT:

✗ a tire iron

✗ pliers

✗ screwdrivers

✗ wrenches

✗ clamps

✗ Allen wrenches

✗ keys

✗ oil cans

✗ a gas can

✗ a tarp

✗ a pan

✗ a coffee mug

✗ a sleeping bag

✗ bungee cords

✗ a fork

✗ matches

A FIRST-AID KIT:

✗ aspirin

✗ bandages

✗ eye drops

✗ antibiotic

✗ scissors

✗ tape

✗ a spoon

Bandages and tape for when she falls, and she will.

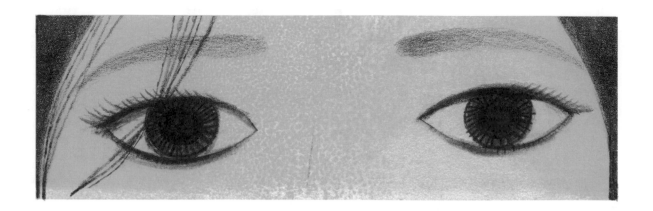

A little voice says, *It's dangerous to go around the world all by yourself.* It says, *You will miss your cat, your clothes, Mozart.*

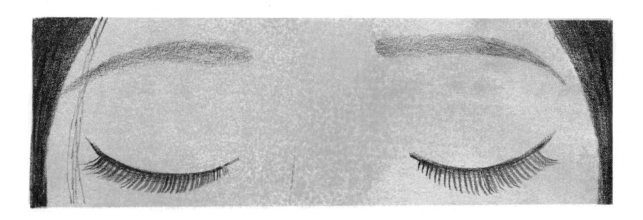

Another voice says, *Be quiet. Listen to the road.*

And so she does. She listens to the road.
And the road says, *Vas. Go.*

She cruises from Etoile to Champs-Élysées.
She loops around the Arc de Triomphe.
She waves au revoir to the Eiffel Tower.

And then she takes off into the world.

CANADA

The girl and her motorcycle take a jumbo jet from Paris to Montreal.
Sometimes the only way to cross an ocean is to fly.
She sends a message back home: *I am alive.*

And then she fills her tank with gas, and she heads west.
The open road is wide and shines like leather.
For days she rides, passing through towns like:
Maniwaki, Michipicoten, Saskatoon.

At night, she parks beneath trees at campgrounds, a good place to sleep. She washes up in service station sinks. Strangers bring her coffee.

Some people smile.

Others stare.

A girl on a motorcycle is a big deal.

After dinner, she sets up her tent
and makes a fire.

HOW TO MAKE A FIRE:

- ✖ Stack the wood like the spokes of a wheel.
- ✖ Make sure the logs are airy: not too high, not too low.
- ✖ Gather kindling.
- ✖ Strike a match and cup it with your hands.
- ✖ Blow gently till the kindling catches.

Morning smells of damp earth, grass, wildflowers.
The air thick with mystery, moss, and strawberries.

She passes snow-capped mountains.
Everything is wild and beautiful.

The farther the girl goes, the fewer
people she sees,

the more trees.

Soon there is no one.
No signs, no cars,
no electric poles.

The road is hers.

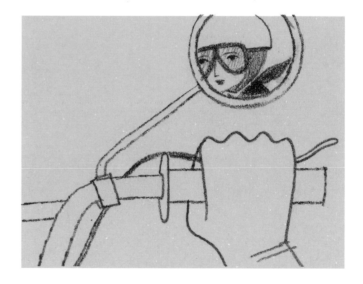

She is all alone, but she is not
afraid. She is *free*.

The stillness is broken only by the
hum of her motorcycle engine.

At the end of the day,
the girl pulls off the road,

dresses up,
and eats

at a roadside diner.

A plate of thick pancakes with extra syrup and butter for a buck.

Some nights it rains.
Drops tap her makeshift tent.
She plays cards and writes to pass the time.

Other nights, it is clear.
And above her, stars sparkle and spin,
planets form, galaxies swirl.

One night in the Yukon
she floats in a warm pool
that glows like a mirror.
She can feel the earth turn.

Above her, aurora borealis.
A whorl of colorful light
connects the girl and heaven.
She closes her eyes. She flies.

At the border between Canada and the United States,
a large sign welcomes her.

The girl and her motorcycle fly from Anchorage to Tokyo.
And from Tokyo, over the Indian Ocean, to Bombay.

INDIA

Bombay is vibrant.

The road charges
with trucks and buses,
rickshaws and
Ambassador cars, cows,
festivals, and . . .

Qu'est-ce que c'est?

Elephants!

Outside of the city, the road opens up.
The sun is warm on the girl's skin.
Her motorcycle's engine purrs.

She rides beside ruby-red passenger trains, waves.
She passes mud houses and carved palaces.

Women in the field, their saris curling
about their feet like flower petals.

Her bike runs out of gas.
Her bike breaks down, needs to be repaired.
When her motorcycle stops, the girl stops.
It takes courage for a girl to live this way.

She finds a shop, waves to mechanics.
Some fix her bike for free.

She pays them with hand-drawn
hearts and handshakes.

HOW TO DRINK TEA IN INDIA:

✗ Tea is called chai.

✗ Chai is milky and sweet.

✗ Drink it from a small clay cup.

✗ Smash the clay cup on the ground when
   you are done.

AFGHANISTAN

Tonight Kabul, soon Kandahar.
Faraway places
the girl once dreamed of.
And now, here you are.

She takes the Khyber Pass.
Some believe the shortest route
from point to point is a straight line.
But the girl and her motorcycle love curves.
When her motorcycle is happy, the girl is happy.

She descends into a lush valley.
A river, wide, fast, and blue as a sapphire, flows beside her.
She takes her heavy boots off and puts her feet
in the cold water.

She crosses a hot, dry desert.
Ribbons of dust unfurl behind her.
Dirt stings her eyes. Sun burns her skin.
Air vibrates with heat.

She falls often.
Sometimes it is fun.
Sometimes not.
But she always gets back up.

She arrives in Kabul at sunset,
everything rose-colored.

She treats herself to a cold drink.

There are no signs on the old road to Bamiyan.
Her motorcycle breaks down again and again going up the last hill.

Sometimes the only way up a hill is to climb.
What awaits at the top is worth it.

Carved into the ancient pearl-colored cliffs above her,
two giant Buddhas, sixteen centuries old.

Inside, there are stairs and rooms,
the sandstone still warm from the day's sun.

The girl climbs from the Buddha's feet up to the top of its head,
where she can see the entire horizon.

The guide leaves her alone.
I wish you all the happiness in the world.

The only sounds: clothes rustling, an insect.
The only sounds: breathing, her heart beating.
It just might be the most beautiful moment
in the girl's life.

It is the end of September. Fall is in the air.
She will need to leave soon. She will never return.
Early in the next century, these Buddhas will be gone.

In Kandahar, the flowers
smell like honey.
A boy gives her a just-picked
pink zinnia.

A child with big gray eyes and red cheeks takes her hand
and shows the girl her school, her home, her family.

At the market, scents of meat, cardamom, cinnamon, gasoline.
The girl bargains for silver jewelry.

At a tea shop, she takes her helmet off, releasing her long brown hair.
She is the only girl there.

She writes letters home. Shares her cake.

Asalaamu alaikum. Walaikum asalaam.

Outside, in the dirt, the girl draws a picture of the Eiffel Tower,
a cloud, and a bird. *Where I am from.*

She spreads a map across a table, a small crowd gathers.
She points: *Where I am. Where I want to go.*

On the way out of town, she blows a tire.
She pulls to the side of the road to patch it.
A truck stops. A group of men steps out.

They help her change her tire.

Her motorcycle is tough, like her.

HOW TO CHANGE A TIRE:

✖ Remove wheel; let air out of tire.

✖ With your boot, loosen and lever the tire from the rim.

✖ Lever new tire onto rim and in the right direction.

✖ Inflate tire.

TURKEY

A pink sunset is a gift to the lone girl on a motorcycle, on the way to Istanbul.

Here, a bridge connects the east to the west.
The girl and her motorcycle cross from one continent to another.
The sea sparkles below her.

One day she will write a book. She will tell the world:
It is hard. It is hot. I learned a lot.

Children run after her bike, shout. *Hello! Hello! Mister! Mister!*

Some are curious, others shy. *Yes, I am a girl.*
Children run after her bike, shout. *Goodbye! Goodbye!*

BULGARIA,

YUGOSLAVIA,

HUNGARY,

AUSTRIA, GERMANY . . .

Whole countries pass by.

Miles and miles of open road.

Time passes. And doesn't.

The girl is mesmerized.

J'ai envie que le monde soit beau, et il est beau.
J'ai envie que les gens soient bons, et ils sont bons.

I want the world to be beautiful, and it is beautiful.
I want people to be good, and they are good.

HOME

Sunburned, bruised, and beaming,
the girl arrives home on a cool, gray day.

Paris is the same and it is different.
She is the same and different, too.

The girl and her motorcycle have traveled thousands of miles.
The pages of her passport are decorated with colorful stamps.

She wears the world like a beautifully embroidered scarf,
all the places she's been, the things she's seen.

The world is beautiful. The world is good.

When she closes her eyes, the girl can still hear the road.
Elsewhere is a just a little bit farther.

To Anne-France Dautheville, merci beaucoup.
To Tamar, for loving this book as much as I do, thank you.
And, for Quinn.
—A.N.

For my dad and for my brothers,
who also put many miles on a Kawasaki dirt bike in 1973.
—J.M.

VIKING
An imprint of Penguin Random House LLC, New York

First published in the United States of America by Viking,
an imprint of Penguin Random House LLC, 2020

Text copyright © 2020 by Amy Novesky
Illustrations copyright © 2020 by Julie Morstad

Visit us online at penguinrandomhouse.com

Viking & colophon is a registered trademark of Penguin Random House LLC.

Library of Congress Cataloging-in-Publication Data is available.
ISBN 9780593116296

1   3   5   7   9   10   8   6   4   2

Design by Nancy Brennan • Set in Futura Handwritten Medium
Artwork was made using pencil, ink, and digital.

Manufactured in China

ABOUT ANNE-FRANCE DAUTHEVILLE

Girl on a Motorcycle is based on and inspired by a real-life girl: Anne-France Dautheville, who was the first woman to ride a motorcycle around the world alone.

In 1972, at the age of twenty-eight, Anne-France left her life in Paris to travel and to write. She wanted to be free and to see the world. And, for the next ten years, she did. On her very first ride—the Orion Raid, a motorcycle tour from Paris, France, to Isfahan, Iran—she was the only woman rider of over one hundred riders. No one believed she would finish, least of all herself. But she did. Still, people doubted her. And so she declared, Je repars, toute seule! "I'm going back, all alone!" And in 1973, she set out again, alone, becoming the first woman to ride across the world solo on a motorcycle. For four months, she rode from Paris across Canada to Alaska, in Japan, through India, Pakistan, Afghanistan, Iran, Turkey, Bulgaria, Yugoslavia, Hungary, Austria, Germany, and back home again. Trips across Australia and South America followed.

Astride a Kawasaki 100cc and a 900cc BMW flat twin, she crossed countries and continents, covered tens of thousands of miles, and collected numerous adventures— flat tires, falls, breakdowns, dangerous storms. She found beauty and good people everywhere she went. And she traveled in effortless style, wearing biker boots and leather coveralls, a helmet and a silk scarf, her long hair down, her eyes always made-up.

As a traveler and as a writer, Anne-France was driven by a deep sense of curiosity and respect. "What can we

Photo credits: © Collection Dautheville

share?" She wanted to give to and share deeply with perfect strangers she met along the way. She wrote articles and books about her travels, including *Une demoiselle sur une moto* and *Et j'ai suivi le vent*, her adventures causing a sensation back home.

Currently, Anne-France Dautheville lives not far from Paris. She no longer rides—she sold her motorcycle at age seventy-two—but she still writes.

AUTHOR'S NOTE

When I saw the rosy photograph of a girl on a motorcycle on the cover of *The New York Times Magazine*, I thought: *Who is this gutsy and gorgeous girl?* And when I read that Anne-France Dautheville was the first woman to ride her motorcycle around the world, in the early 1970s, I had that rare sparkly feeling: *I want to write this story.*

The idea of a girl on a motorcycle traveling alone around the world captured many feelings I feel: about being a girl, about the world, about being a girl in the world, about being a girl sending her child out into the world. In one of Anne-France's books about her travels, she writes: J'ai envie que le monde soit beau, et il est beau. J'ai envie que les gens soient bons, et ils sont bons. "I want the world to be beautiful, and it is beautiful. I want people to be good, and they are good." I fell in love with Anne-France on the spot. It didn't hurt that she is a writer, too. And from Paris, to boot.

C'est tout. I contacted Anne-France, wrote the story, and jumped on a CDG-bound plane from San Francisco, where I met a real-life heroine. Unlike Anne-France, I am not a gutsy traveler. It took a lot for me to board that plane and travel halfway around the world, alone. But I knew I had to do it, especially for this book. And because I believe you have to get on that motorbike or that jet plane, even (and especially) if you are afraid, and live your life.

What Anne-France and I do share is how fortunate we are to be able to travel the world, to come and go as we please, to easefully cross borders. And for that, I am deeply humbled. The world was a different place when Anne-France roamed it. I've tried to be as true to her story and as respectful to the people and places she visited as I can.

What I wish for all young citizens of the world, for every human being on this incredible planet, is the ability and freedom to travel, to wander, and to lust for elsewhere, to meet people, to experience through their own eyes and hearts that the world is beautiful and good. Because I believe, dear reader, that it is.